— THE RESCUE SERIES

Al The Alpaca

Forever Friends

DIANE ODEGARD GOCKEL

ISBN: 0989631729
ISBN 13: 9780989631723

Diane Odegard Gockel is a former high school teacher who has devoted much of her life to the rescue, fostering and adoption of homeless pets. She and her daughter Julie Diane Stafford co-own Creative Kids Unplugged. Diane and her husband have four grown children and live on a small farm in Sammamish, Washington called Second Chance Ranch.

**Other books in the Rescue Series by
Diane Odegard Gockel**

The Rescue of Winks

Bella Saves the Farm

Fancy Has a Plan

I'm Al the alpaca, a name given to me by the Farm Lady later in my life. Before I met her, I lived on an alpaca ranch with so many alpacas that we were never even given names. My youth was spent being lazy, grazing in the lush, green pastures, and playing with my alpaca buddies, who were later named Francis and Teddy Bear.

Although I was the oldest, we all agreed that Francis was the wisest and the greatest of all storytellers. He was a pure-white alpaca, often quiet, but he always seemed to command a leadership role. Each summer night, as all the other alpacas would head for shelter and sleep in the nearby sheds or under trees, my alpaca friends and I would sleep under the starry sky and listen to the many riveting stories that Francis shared. My favorite story was the tale Francis called "Forever Friends," a story about the adventures of two young alpacas that remained friends for life.

Teddy Bear was the youngest, but least cautious, of all of us. He had no problem introducing himself to anyone. He also had the most ideas about what was fun, and he always got us playing and laughing. He was a dark-brown, nearly black alpaca with eyes that matched his hair, which made it hard to know sometimes whether he was coming or going. He took the boredom out of everything and loved to play tricks on the other alpacas.

As spring left us and summer began to burst into bloom, many of the alpacas on the ranch began to be taken away. The rumor was that the ranch would soon be sold, and all the alpacas must move to new homes and new places. None of us knew when that day would come for us, and although we never wanted to talk much about it, we knew it was just a matter of time. I was only hoping that we could all stay together.

Early one morning, after waking up and starting to enjoy a bit of breakfast, a large truck stopped by our pasture, and the ranch people started pointing my way. Soon they haltered me up, pulled me into the back of a truck, and took me away from the life I had known as an alpaca kid. I remember the loss of joy in Teddy Bear's face as he watched the ranchers' truck bouncing down the gravel road, taking me to a life of unknowns. But what I remember most was the courage on Francis's face as he yelled toward the truck, "Forever friends."

Over the next couple of days, I was traded a few times and moved from truck to shed and back to truck, and finally I landed on what appeared to be a sheep farm. This place made me uncomfortable and fearful. This was partly because I was the only alpaca but also because of the way the sheep ranch was run. All the sheep were crammed in this small barn with only two stalls. Each day, the ranchers would take away several sheep at a time and bring them to another building, never to be seen again. It was just me surrounded by so many sheep that I didn't even have enough room to lay down and rest my legs. They never fed us grass or hay—just straw.

Occasionally, a goat would find its way to the sheep ranch, but within a few days a lady would show up, load the goat in her truck, and rush off. They were the lucky ones. The Goat Lady always seemed to notice me and even asked the ranchers questions about me, but I was always left with the sheep.

One day, the Goat Lady showed up with another large vehicle following her. Again, she loaded her truck with a few lucky goats. Then, coming out of the other vehicle, I saw the Farm Lady and Man for the first time. The Goat Lady was chatting with them, and the Rancher then pointed my way.

The Rancher, an old, gruff man, was never gentle, and he seemed to have no feelings for us. He walked up to me, slapped a halter on my head, and dragged me out of the sheep pen where I had been standing for months. I hadn't even realized how filthy and sore I had become. My beautiful, white hair was caked in mud and straw. I was a mess. The Rancher dragged me over to the farmers' truck, shoved me in the back, and slammed the gate closed. It was silent. Where was I going? Was this the end for me?

My breathing began to calm when the Farm Lady and Man entered the large car, shut the doors, and started the engine. The Farm Lady was gentle and kind. She turned and talked to me in a slow, peaceful voice as the three of us exited the ranch gates. I watched out the back window as the ranch got farther and farther away. Then I did something I had not done in quite a while; I lay down. I didn't have any idea where I was going, but I knew it could not be worse than the place I just left.

We drove for quite a long time, and the Farm Lady talked to me for most of the ride. That's when she gave me my first name: "I shall call you Al," she said, "Al the alpaca." Having a name made me feel important, like I belonged and was loved. It was nearly sunset and it would soon get dark outside, which made me so homesick for the alpaca ranch of my youth and the starlit sky I had shared with my alpaca companions. As we reached our destination, the Farm Lady got out and opened a large gate as the Farm Man drove through. Our vehicle then came to a halt, and the Farm Man got out too. Soon, the back door slowly opened, and the Farm Lady slowly hooked a lead rope to my halter and gently nudged me out.

It was then that I got my first glorious look at the farm. Rolling hills of rich, green grass! I instantly grabbed a quick bite, and I knew I had not tasted anything that delicious in a long time. I looked at the hill and saw a small barn next to the water trough, and that's when I saw five goats running straight toward me, playfully tossing their heads. Patrick, a big, white goat was the largest and clearly the leader, and seemed to be very curious about me. I was cautious but interested in my new pasture mates.

The Farm Lady unhooked the lead rope and halter and gave me the go ahead to explore my surroundings. I took off in a trot. It felt so good to move again! The goats and I headed up to the barn as the last of the daylight was replaced by a cool and glorious night. The goats slept in the barn that night, but not me; I slept out under the stars.

The next day I got up with the sun. I couldn't wait to enjoy the rich grass that I had missed for so long. I ate and ate and ate until I was so full that I lay down on the crest of the hill and looked out over the farm. In an adjacent pasture, I saw a brown-and-white and a solid white horse, a couple of miniature donkeys, and two llamas out enjoying the beauty of the morning. There were even a couple of border collies, Chase and Bella, patrolling the fence line. Patrick told me all the names of the animals on the farm. This was truly a peaceful place.

Weeks passed, and I began to put weight back on and gain the strength I had lost. The Farm Lady took excellent care of us. From time to time, she would bring the farm vehicle through the gates and drop off a goat that would stay with us until it found a new home of its own. Although Patrick and I became fast friends, there were moments when I really missed my alpaca friends. Francis's last words to me, "Forever friends" rested in my heart. I knew that even though we were no longer together, we would always be forever friends.

One sunny afternoon, the Goat Lady drove up the long driveway. I had not seen her since my days at the sheep ranch. She got out and visited with the Farm Lady. I watched them curiously as they grabbed a couple of lead ropes and opened up the back of the goat truck. More goats, I thought. That's when I saw a familiar face emerge from the back of the truck. Teddy Bear! Oh my goodness! I started to dash toward the gate to greet my dear friend when I saw Francis's head pop out and his legs touch ground. I could not believe my little alpaca eyes! Joy swirled through me!

The Farm Lady escorted Francis and Teddy Bear to the pasture gate. Teddy Bear looked scared and unsure. Francis was putting up a brave front for Teddy Bear, but I could tell he was frightened too. As the gate opened, the Farm Lady announced to them, "This will be your forever home." Teddy Bear and Francis suddenly spotted me for the first time since they'd arrived. Shock and joy filled their faces!

"I can't believe it's you!" cried Teddy Bear. "Together again!" cheered Francis.

As quick as the Farm Lady could unhook their lead ropes, the three of us trotted up the hill, tossing our heads and playing like old times. We rolled in the grass, and I got to introduce them to Patrick and the others.

As night fell and the goats headed to the barn, my forever friends and I found a great spot under the starry sky, and Francis told us stories.

The real Al, Francis and Teddy Bear, after

shearing.

The real Al leaving sheep farm.

Made in the USA
Coppell, TX
12 August 2020